HOT TOPICS

SUPERBUGS

John DiConsiglio

www.raintreepublishers.co.uk
Visit our website to find out
more information about
Raintree books.

To order:
☎ Phone 0845 6044371
📠 Fax +44 (0) 1865 312263
📠 Email myorders@raintreepublishers.co.uk

Customers from outside the UK please telephone +44 1865 312262

Raintree is an imprint of Capstone Global Library
Limited, a company incorporated in England and
Wales having its registered office at 7 Pilgrim
Street, London, EC4V 6LB – Registered company
number: 6695582

Edited by Adam Miller, Nick Hunter, and
  Diyan Leake
Designed by Philippa Jenkins
Original illustrations © Capstone Global
  Library Ltd 2012
Picture research by Mica Brancic
Production by Eirian Griffiths and Alison Parsons
Originated by Capstone Global Library Ltd
Printed and bound in China by Leo Paper
  Products Ltd

ISBN 978 1 406 23504 3
15 14 13 12 11
10 9 8 7 6 5 4 3 2 1

British Library Cataloguing in Publication Data
DiConsiglio, John
Superbugs – (Hot Topics)
616.9'041-dc22
A full catalogue record for this book is available
from the British Library.

Acknowledgements
We would like to thank the following for
permission to reproduce photographs: Corbis
pp. 15 (© Bettmann), 19 (© Visuals Unlimited),
43 (© Karen Kasmauski); Getty Images p. 11
(AFP Photo/Belga/Jorge Dirkx); Infectious
Diseases Society of America/Amber Don p. 7; PA
Archive p. 35 (Press Association Images/© Care
Quality Commission); Photoshot p. 51 (© Xinhua/
Liu Haifeng); Bo Salisbury p. 21; Science Photo
Library pp. 17 top (A. Dowsett, Health Protection
Agency), 23 (Custom Medical Stock Photo/
Bryson Biomedical Illustration), 29 (Dr Gary
Gaugler), 31 (James King-Holmes), 36 (Paul
Gunning), 53 (CDC); Shutterstock pp. 4 (© Hiper
Com), 9 (© Leonid Shcheglov), 16 (© Sebastian
Kaulitzki), 25 (© Margarita Borodina), 33
(© Alexander Raths), 41 (© aquariagirl1970), 48
(© Anthony DiChello), 55 (© Nanka); Shutterstock
pp. 17 bottom (© Sebastian Kaulitzki), 17 middle
bottom (© Sebastian Kaulitzki), 17 middle top
(© Sebastian Kaulitzki), 38 (Fotonium).

Cover photograph of Methicillin-resistant
Staphylococcus aureus (MRSA) on the
microscopic fibres of a wound dressing
reproduced with permission of Science Photo
Library (Paul Gunning).

Every effort has been made to contact copyright
holders of material reproduced in this book.
Any omissions will be rectified in subsequent
printings if notice is given to the publishers.

CONTENTS

Some words are printed in bold, **like this**. You can find out what they mean by looking in the glossary.

HUMANS VS BUGS

It was a real-life medical mystery that had doctors baffled. In the summer of 2010, three patients in three different states in the United States were admitted to hospitals with mysterious ailments. They had the same **symptoms**: gut and urinary **infections**, painful stomach cramps, fever, and nausea. Otherwise, they had little in common. One patient was a woman from California who had been in a car accident. Another was a man from Illinois with a long history of medical problems. The third was a woman from Massachusetts suffering from cancer.

For decades, physicians have fought bacteria with antibiotics. But new superbugs have baffled even the best doctors.

WHAT'S BUGGING YOU?

In this book, you will see many references to the word *bug* or even *superbug*. But we are not talking about ants or spiders – and certainly not a Super Mosquito with a big red cape. No, this book is about bacteria, **viruses**, all the nasty bugs that can make you sick. Have you ever heard someone say they caught a nasty flu bug? They do not mean they trapped a horrible moth in a jar. They mean a virus invaded their body and gave them influenza. Those are the bugs you will meet when you turn the page.

The unbeatable bug

Each of the patients had contracted a strong infection. The ailments were caused by **bacteria**. Bacteria are microscopic, single-cell "bugs" and they are the most abundant life forms on Earth. Physicians knew how to fight bacteria. Their main weapon was a type of drug called **antibiotics**. These powerful medicines had successfully destroyed bad bacteria for decades. The medical world has relied on antibiotics for a long time to protect against everything from nasty cuts and scrapes to killer bacterial diseases.

Doctors gave the three patients a normal dose of antibiotics. Then they waited to watch the symptoms subside. But nothing happened. The ill people became more ill. Doctors tried a stronger antibiotic. But it proved as useless as the first drug.

The physicians were stunned. The bacteria seemed to brush off the antibiotics. Medicine's strongest weapon had no effect on the mystery bug. As doctors huddled over their patients, they began to realize exactly how frightening their new enemy might be.

This was no ordinary bacterium. This was a superbug. That meant an **infectious** disease nightmare – and a worldwide crisis.

A global pandemic?

Soon, word spread from scientists around the world. This super-strong bacteria was not just a problem for the United States. From Canada to the United Kingdom, from Japan to India, hospitals were reporting more cases of the strange infection. And none of them could be cured with antibiotics.

About 1.2 million hospital patients a year get bacterial infections – and 90,000 of them die. In the United Kingdom alone, antibiotic-resistant bug-related deaths have risen sharply, from fewer than 100 annually in the 1990s to more than 1,600 throughout the 2000s. The US National Institute of Allergy and Infectious Diseases estimates that more than 70 per cent of the bacteria that cause these infections are resistant to one or more antibiotics. In 2006, Maribel Espaba, a 33-year-old British nurse, died of a superbug-related pneumonia just five days after giving birth to her first child. Doctors believed she contracted the disease from a patient while working in the diabetic ward at the University Hospital of North Staffordshire.

One of the most common superbugs is called **MRSA**. It got its name by defeating an antibiotic called **methicillin**. The bug that causes MRSA infections is called *Staphylococcus aureus*. MRSA stands for "methicillin-resistant *Staphylococcus aureus*". Doctors expect to see MRSA in hospitals and nursing homes but it is also common in the outside world.

Virulent MRSA has even killed healthy people. In January 2007, Carlos Don, a young school boy from California, was diagnosed with the flu. When his symptoms got worse, his parents rushed him to hospital. His heart, lungs, and other organs were fatally damaged. When he died in February 2007, doctors determined that the cause of death was MRSA.

WHAT DO YOU THINK?

Anyone can get a superbug but they are usually found in hospitals. Have you ever stayed overnight in hospital? Did doctors or nurses talk to you about bacterial infections? How do you think hospitals try to stop superbugs from spreading to patients? Do you think there is anything you can do to keep yourself safe?

In January 2007, young Carlos Don was diagnosed with the flu. But as his organs failed, it was clear he was sick with something much worse. Weeks later, he died from MRSA.

MRSA is the most common antibiotic-resistant bug in the world – from Europe and the Americas to North Africa, the Middle East, and East Asia. As worldwide travel became more common in the last few decades, the bug spread quickly around the world by sick passengers carrying a superbug in their systems.

In 1967, a tribe in New Guinea was struck down by a virulent pneumonia that was impervious to an antibiotic called **penicillin**. This was the outbreak of the first widespread superbug on record. In England, infection by the super *Clostridium difficile* (**C. diff**) – a bacterial gut infection that mainly affects the elderly – was blamed for more than 300 hospital deaths in the mid-2000s. Today, some Iraq War veterans are coming home with a drug-resistant infection caused by *Acinetobacter.* This bug enters through the soldiers' wounds and has often meant that the infected limbs have had to be amputated. **Tuberculosis (TB),** which is among the world's most deadly infectious diseases, is also becoming increasingly antibiotic-resistant. TB kills two million people worldwide each year.

Scientists are fighting to stay ahead of the killer bugs. They are searching for new drugs to stop the bacteria onslaught. In doing so, they have come to a horrible realization. Superbugs became indestructible because of us.

How humans created superbugs

Since their discovery and widespread use in the 1940s, antibiotics had kept the world's deadliest bugs, from **meningitis** to pneumonia, at bay. The battle against bacteria seemed to be over – and humankind had won.

But almost immediately after doctors started using antibiotics, they noticed a frightening characteristic of disease-causing bacteria. The bugs can **mutate** – or change – their basic **genetic structure**. Over time, they grow resistant to drugs that once wiped them out. They become superbugs – bacteria that are incredibly hard, or even impossible, to kill.

Each time you take an antibiotic, the weakest bugs are killed instantly. But the strongest bacteria – perhaps one in ten million – adapt to the presence of the drug. Superbugs adapt in order to beat the drug and then multiply. They can even pass their drug-resistant adaptation on to other bacteria in the body. One tiny microbe can produce an army of superbugs.

ALL IN THE GENES

Every living thing has **genes**. Genes are like instruction manuals for our bodies, which exist in **DNA**. They act as the proteins that make our bodies function. They also determine our individual characteristics such as whether we will have blue or brown eyes. Each cell in the human body contains about 25,000 to 35,000 genes.

Depending on the species, bacteria can have anything from 575 to 5,500 genes, much fewer than humans. But, just as with people, genes hold the blueprints for how bacteria will act. Under normal circumstances, when a bacterial gene is sending the right instructions to the organism, it may direct the bacteria to wither against an antibiotic's attack. But a gene can mutate. The gene mutates itself in order to survive. In effect, the gene sends new instructions to its host bacteria: not to succumb to the antibiotic, but to destroy it.

COLDS AND FLU

The best way you can protect yourself against bacteria is by using antibiotics correctly. Over 90 per cent of cases of colds, sore throats, and earaches are caused by viruses, not bacteria. Antibiotics do not work against viruses. You should begin to feel better over time thanks to your body's **immune system** doing its job. Let your doctor know you do not want an antibiotic unless it is absolutely necessary.

In many cases, antibiotics are still necessary to save lives. But experts say we depend far too heavily on these drugs. In 1954, nearly one million kilograms of antibiotics were produced in the United States. By 2000, that number had risen to nearly 23 million kilograms.

In **developed countries** such as the United Kingdom, patients need a doctor's **prescription** to get antibiotics such as penicillin. In **developing countries** such as India, antibiotics are widely available in shops. This is a serious problem because it makes it almost impossible to control antibiotic use.

However, people are not the biggest overusers of antibiotics. They are widely given to livestock on farms and in slaughterhouses. Some are used to fend off diseases. Others are used to promote fast growth in pigs, cows, and chickens. But superbugs can develop in animals, too. Scientists are worried that food-borne bugs can end up on people's plates.

Antibiotics are used to prevent illness in animals that are intensively farmed.

CASE STUDY

Bringing the superbug home

In the summer of 2010, doctors in the United States struggled to identify the new mystery bug that was making patients sick. Antibiotics were not working for the car accident victim from California, the frail man from Illinois, or the cancer patient from Massachusetts.

Those cases were not isolated. An unknown gene was turning many types of bacteria into superbugs, resistant to nearly all antibiotics. The bug had spread around the world. Reports were coming in from Australia, Canada, the Netherlands, the United Kingdom, Japan, and Sweden. But the centre of the crisis was India. In fact, the bug was already named **NDM-1**, after the Indian city of New Delhi where it was first spotted.

In poor countries, people often have limited access to clean drinking water or adequate sewage systems. That makes them a prime breeding ground for bacterial diseases. But how did three Americans, more than two dozen Britons, and a host of others catch a bug that originated in India?

Nearly all of the sick people had recently travelled to India for medical tourism. This is when people from countries such as the United Kingdom and United States travel to countries such as India, Pakistan, and Thailand for surgical treatments because they are cheaper. In each case, the tourists risked contracting a drug-resistant bug. NDM-1 was particularly frightening, especially as it could spread from hand to mouth.

So far, cases of NDM-1 infection are few. Only one death is directly linked to the bug. In August 2010, a Belgian man caught NDM-1 in a Pakistan hospital after a car accident. He was given a powerful antibiotic called colistin. But the drug was useless against the superbug. Doctors watched helplessly as the infection killed their patient.

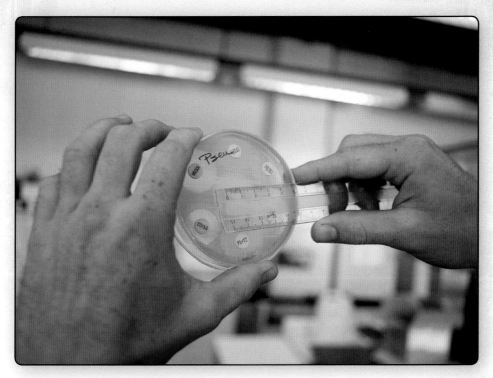
Scientists study bacteria in Petri dishes. They can examine the way that bugs such as NDM-1 mutate into drug-resistant strains.

Some doctors say there is no reason to panic. Massachusetts doctors involved in the case hope that "with good infection control … [NDM-1] can be held at bay". They advise people not to overreact. But many warn that a superbug may just be the tip of an epidemic iceberg.

MEDICAL TOURISM SPREADS SUPERBUGS

In India, Pakistan, and Thailand, medical tourism is a booming business, growing by as much as 30 per cent a year. On average, medical costs in India are one-fifth lower than in the United Kingdom and the United States. But when these patients return home, they may bring the superbug back with them. Scientists believe that is how NDM-1 spread from India to Massachusetts – and how new and ever more dangerous bacteria will spread around the world.

Good bugs, bad bugs

Bacteria are not always the enemy. In fact, we could not survive without them.

Bacteria can live in soil and water. But animals are their best homes, providing the moisture and food they need to live. The human body is teeming with different types of bacteria. Millions live on our skin as well as in our respiratory and intestinal tracts. There are ten times as many bacteria in the human gut as there are cells in your entire body.

Most of the bacteria are friendly. "Good" bacteria fend off diseases. They make your immune system stronger, produce vitamins, and even help you to digest your food. Outside the body, bacteria help to keep our environment clean. Bacteria recycle nutrients from dead animals and plants and even convert toxic waste into harmless products.

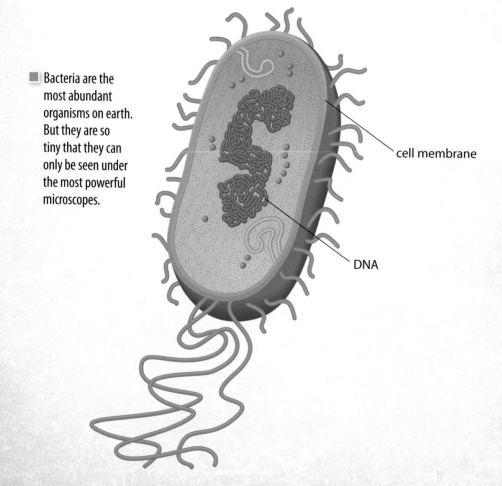

Bacteria are the most abundant organisms on earth. But they are so tiny that they can only be seen under the most powerful microscopes.

cell membrane

DNA

"Bad" bacteria usually live outside your body. They may even be fine as long as they're not in a part of your body where they can cause problems. They can cause diseases in people and animals such as the throat condition known as strep throat, cholera, and whooping cough. Bad bacteria can enter your body through your mouth and nose and lead to infections in your digestive system and lungs. The bacteria that cause tuberculosis, for example, are inhaled in moisture droplets. Other bacteria, such as *E. coli* and *Streptococcus pyogenes*, can lead to food poisoning.

Dangerous bacteria can also get into your body through skin cuts or grazes. That can set off blood poisoning or tissue destruction. The flesh-eating disease known as **necrotizing fasciitis (NF)** is caused by the same bacteria, *Streptococcus* A, that produces common infections such as strep throat.

Before antibiotics, some of the most common bacterial diseases killed millions of people. Epidemics of plague, tuberculosis, and leprosy wiped out whole civilizations. The Black Death, a plague caused by bacteria and spread by the fleas on rats, killed 30 to 60 per cent of Europe's population in just two years during the 14th century. It was not a very powerful bug, but because there were no antibiotics, it reduced the world's population from 450 million to as little as 350 million in 1400. Even today, tuberculosis kills 1.8 million people a year, and 20 per cent of tuberculosis cases are drug-resistant superbugs. With antibiotics, science was certain it had finally gained the upper hand against bad bacteria. But science had got it wrong.

BACTERIA FACTS

- Three of the main types of infections killing people today are caused by bacteria: tuberculosis, whooping cough, and tetanus.
- Many bacteria can only be seen under the most powerful microscopes. They are so small that 2.5 billion bacteria can be found in one gram of soil.
- Bacteria can be used to make food such as cheese and yoghurt.

INSIDE SCIENCE

Imagine it is 1941. You have had a bad fall on your bicycle and broken your ankle. A surgeon repairs the damage but a nasty bacterial infection gets inside a cut on your leg. Within days, you lie near comatose, your fever reaching 105 degrees.

Doctors have often watched helplessly as young people died from minor wounds. In desperation, they decide to try a new medicine. They inject it into your veins every few hours. In a few days, you have completely recovered.

Miracle drugs

For years, people referred to the new medicine as the miracle drug. But it was really a triumph of science. The drug was called penicillin and it was the world's first antibiotic.

Today, it is hard to imagine what life would be like without antibiotics. In the past, children could die from strep throats. Appendicitis was deadly. Soldiers routinely died from infections that got inside their wounds.

Antibiotics are powerful medications that target dangerous bacteria as they attack our bodies. Many antibiotics are made from natural sources such as fungi and bacteria. Others are **synthetic**, created in laboratories. When they are properly prescribed, antibiotics work with your body's own natural defences to fight against invading bacteria. They kill bacteria in different ways. Some antibiotics dissolve the protective cell wall of a bacteria, rupturing and killing it. Others enter the bacteria and break down its DNA structure. That stops the bug from making essential proteins and reproducing itself into an army of germs. Once the antibiotic breaks down the invading bacteria, your body's immune system takes over and nurses you back to health.

HOW ONE FUNGUS SAVED MILLIONS OF LIVES

By the early 20th century, medical science knew a lot about the tiny organisms called bacteria that caused infections. In 1660, Dutch cloth merchant Antonie van Leeuwenhoek was the first to see bacteria. He was grinding magnifying lenses to examine the weave of his cloth. When he used his new lenses to look at a sample of pond water, he discovered that one drop was teeming with bacteria. By 1870, the German scientist/physician Robert Koch had shown that some bacteria caused illnesses.

Bacteria – and the illnesses they caused – were no secret to the scientific world. But no one knew how to stop them. Then a Scottish researcher named Alexander Fleming made an accidental discovery that would save millions of lives.

Fleming had seen the horrors of infection during World War I. Infections from even small battlefield wounds killed many soldiers. For years, Fleming worked without success to find a medicine that killed bacteria. He grew sample bacteria in small plates called Petri dishes as he searched for an answer.

One night in 1928, Fleming left his bacteria-filled Petri dishes uncovered near an open window. A few days later, he found strange, empty circles in the dishes. Stray fungus had blown through the window on to the dishes. To Fleming's shock, it killed the bacteria. The fungus, called *Penicillium notatum*, similar to bread mould, would be used to make penicillin. It was the first antibiotic.

Alexander Fleming's accidental discovery would save millions of lives.

The bug strikes back

By 1943, drug companies began producing penicillin in mass quantities. The wonder drug was saving thousands of lives.

However, as early as 1945, Alexander Fleming warned that overusing penicillin was dangerous. He believed it could lead to mutant bacteria that resist the drug's effects.

Bacteria multiply at astounding rates. Just one bug can reproduce a billion times in a single day. Among that group, one in every thousand will have a mutation in its genetic structure – and any one of those mutations could be the one that allows it to resist antibiotics. Experts think that once a bug becomes resistant to one antibiotic, it is easier for it to build resistance to another.

In 1961, MRSA first appeared in UK hospitals, just one year after the antibiotic methicillin was introduced. In 1967, the first penicillin-resistant pneumonia strain was reported in New Guinea. By 1992, about 5 per cent of all bacteria tested in the United States was resistant to penicillin.

Today, as many as 70 per cent of all bacteria are thought to be resistant to at least one antibiotic. As antibiotic use grows, the bugs become more resistant. The more an antibiotic is taken, the easier a superbug can mutate to withstand it.

WANTED DEAD, NOT ALIVE
GET TO KNOW THE NAMES, THEY ARE THE DEADLIEST BACTERIA ON EARTH.

E. COLI

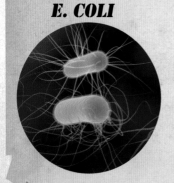

Most strains of *E. coli* are not bad. However, some are a common cause of disease. *E. coli* are commonly found in cattle faeces. Worldwide, more than ten million children die each year from *E. coli*-related diarrhoeal infections. In May 2011, infections of a new strain of *E. coli* broke out in Germany. Within a month, 3,255 people had been become ill, and 35 of these had died.

TUBERCULOSIS

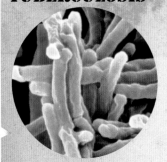

Mycobacterium tuberculosis has ravaged the world for centuries. Once thought to be contained, new antibiotic-resistant strains have led to two million TB deaths a year, mostly in developing countries. TB can lie dormant for years in the respiratory system before becoming active. A third of the world's population is infected with TB.

STREPTOCOCCUS

Streptococcus pneumoniae is largely responsible for pneumonia and bacterial meningitis, which kills nearly 175,000 people a year. *Streptococcus* accounts for as many as one million deaths among children annually. Our bodies have a normal amount of strep in the respiratory system. But it can change into a killer bacterium.

STAPHYLOCOCCUS

Staphylococcus is normally found in small amounts on your skin. In the past, antibiotics cured most cases of this bacteria, but it has now emerged as an antibiotic-resistant superbug. Most cases of MRSA are found in hospitals. But it can be found elsewhere. Community-associated MRSA (CA-MRSA) has become the most frequent cause of skin and soft tissue infections at Accident and Emergency departments.

SALMONELLA

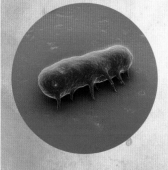

Salmonella causes food poisoning. It lives in the gut of many animals and can affect meat, eggs, poultry, and milk. Green vegetables, fruit, and shellfish which have become contaminated with animal faeces in the soil or water can also transmit *Salmonella* to humans who eat them. For most people, *Salmonella* results in diarrhoea, abdominal cramps, and fever. In 2010, more than 9,100 cases of *Salmonella* infection were reported in the United Kingdom. In some countries, death of victims of *Salmonella* poisoning is as high as 60 per cent.

CASE STUDY

Beware: flesh-eating disease

Bo Salisbury was a 60-year-old postmaster from California, USA. On Saturday afternoons, he played indoor football with teenagers from his church. Saturday 9 May 1998 was a normal Saturday. Bo had a cold, but that did not stop him from playing in goal. He saved a teenager's shot. However, the boy's football boot scraped Bo's ankle. Bo limped off the field with a stinging bruise. A few hours later, the pain was worse. Bo took some aspirin and went to lunch at a Chinese restaurant. By 2 p.m., the pain in his ankle was unbearable.

Bo went to an Accident and Emergency department. A doctor examined the red scratch. He told Bo it was just a nasty sports injury, gave him some painkillers and sent him home

By the next afternoon, Bo was in terrible pain. His ankle had swollen and was horribly reddened. He was nauseous and sweating. His blood pressure was dropping fast. His organs were shutting down. By the time he returned to the hospital, Bo was dying.

Although the doctors did not know it at the time, fatal bacteria had entered Bo's body through the bruise on his ankle, causing a disease called necrotizing fasciitis (NF). It is better known by its headline-grabbing nickname: flesh-eating bacteria.

NF is a rare infection, but the chance of dying from the illness is very high. Between 500 and 1,500 people get it each year, with as many as 30 per cent dying from it. That percentage makes NF one of the most lethal bacteria in the world. Unlike other bacteria, NF does not affect mainly sick people with a weakened immune system. Flesh-eating bacteria can strike anyone at any time.

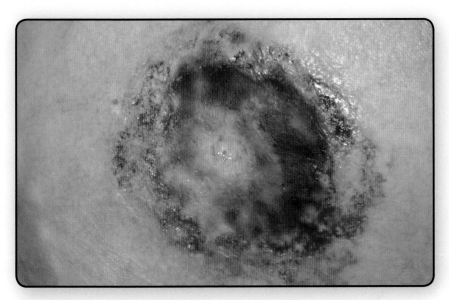

Necrotizing fasciitis destroys the soft tissue below the skin. It can even spark an infection that spreads through the blood and damages lungs and other organs.

A number of bacteria can trigger NF. Bo's disease was caused by *Streptococcus pyogenes*, the same bacteria that leads to strep throat and impetigo. In 2008, British TV personality Ben Fogle suffered from a similar flesh-eating bug. His condition was eventually staved off with antibiotics. But experts say they are seeing more and more flesh-eating bacteria stimulated by MRSA – the antibiotic-resistant bacteria that once were confined to hospitals have now broken out into wider communities.

Bo was a tricky case. He was in good health. He appeared to have nothing wrong with him. But he was clearly dying. His doctor examined his leg. The skin had turned a sickening blue-grey. At first, his doctor thought a blood clot was cutting off the circulation. Maybe his leg was dying from a lack of blood flow.

But tests revealed the presence of the *Streptococcus* bacteria. The bacteria secrete toxins (poisons) that destroy fascia, the soft tissue below your skin. The poisons spread up Bo's leg, rapidly eating away at tissue as it travelled towards his lungs and heart. As Bo's doctor at the University of California-Davis Medical Center said, "This thing travels fast. In 72 hours, you kill it – or it kills you."

Most disease bacteria come from outside your body. But NF is different. As many as 15 to 30 per cent of all people carry the strep bacteria in their bodies. Most have no symptoms at all. But they can pass the bacteria to others, even through tiny cuts or bruises. In addition to damaging the soft tissue below the skin, NF can hasten a more dangerous infection that spreads through the blood to the lungs and other organs.

Bo knew things were not going well. The fatal bacteria was eating its way up his leg, sucking oxygen from his tissue. As he slipped in and out of consciousness, he prepared himself for death. He told his teenage daughter not to cry. He even made her promise to study for her final exams. "There's nothing anyone can do for me now," Bo said.

FLESH-EATING DISEASE

- NF can enter your body through the tiniest cut or bruise. Although it is rare, people have caught the disease from paper cuts, staple punctures, and even pin pricks!

- *Streptococcus* A – one of the bacteria that can cause NF – is present in 15 to 30 per cent of people. Most carry it without knowing it or showing any symptoms, or they may get an infection other than NF, such as strep throat.

- There is not much you can do to protect yourself against NF. Practising good **hygiene** and washing your hands will decrease your chances of catching it. But NF is extremely rare. You probably come into contact with a strep carrier every day, yet only 500 people become sick from it each year.

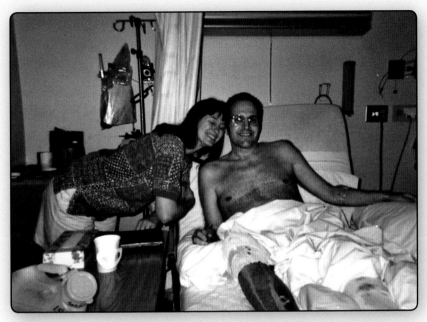

Bo was wrong. There was still hope. Antibiotics were useless against the fast-moving bug. But two hours after his ambulance roared into the University of California-Davis car park, Bo was in surgery. Surgeons raced the infection as it spread up Bo's leg. They sliced off the infected tissue, removing all the flesh from the tip of his toe to the top of his hip.

Remarkably, Bo beat the flesh-eating bacteria. He survived – and did not lose his leg. It was not easy. He underwent skin grafts. Doctors peeled flesh from other parts of his body to replace the skin they cut from his leg. Today, Bo runs 5 kilometres (3 miles) a day. He even competed in a 5-kilometre race. His doctor believes Bo's survival was partly luck – and partly good teamwork. As she put it, "If it were two hours later, he wouldn't have made it."

Bugs at work – how do superbugs beat antibiotics?

How do superbugs actually work? Scientists have singled out a few traits that help bad bacteria evolve into dangerous diseases.

Reinforcements – Bacteria can evolve quickly because they reproduce at such rapid rates. There are about 2,000 species of identified bacteria and probably at least that number again that scientists have yet to identify. The entire bacteria population doubles as often as every 20 minutes. The human population generally doubles every 20 years!

Mutant madness – Bacteria have lived on Earth for 3.5 billion years. They could never have survived that long without a helping hand from Mother Nature. Bugs can mutate their genetic make-up and evolve in ways that let them fight off their enemies. It is a natural defence mechanism. Scientists believe that antibiotics, which are intended to kill the bugs, actually make them mutate faster! The more bacteria are under attack, the more active they become – mutating and passing along their new genes at great speed.

Some bacteria have mutated to harden their surfaces to block entry points for antibiotics. Others produce enzymes, which are proteins that degrade or deactivate the antibiotics, making them useless against disease. Still others actually develop a molecular pump. It catches the antibiotics as they enter the cell membrane (thin "skin" around the cell) and almost immediately spits them out before they can kill off the bacterium.

Trading places – Bacteria can pass their resistant genes on to other bacteria, even if they are a completely different species. The strongest resistance is acquired from short stretches of DNA called **plasmids**. A plasmid can carry the genes that cause antibiotic resistance. It can move from one type of bacteria to another. A single plasmid can pass on several different resistances. In 1968, more than 12,000 people in Guatemala died from a diarrhoea epidemic. The bug had a plasmid that was resistant to four different types of antibiotics.

Can drugs kill good bugs?

Not all bacteria are bad. And not everything an antibiotic does is good. Your body is teeming with millions of friendly bacteria. They grow on your skin, in your mouth and nose, and in your digestive system.

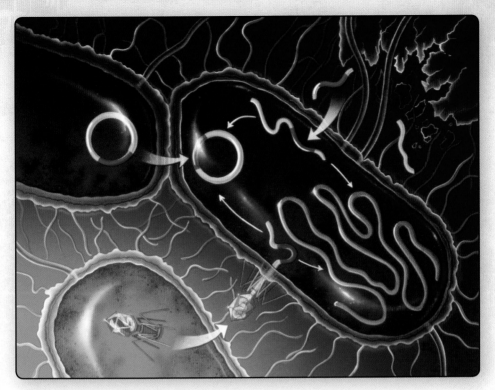
Bacteria have many methods to beat antibiotics. One way is to pass their drug-resistant genes back and forth to each other, even if they are different types of bacteria.

Good bacteria have important jobs in your body. Your intestines are rich with good bacteria that help you digest your food. Good bacteria also carry out the important function of crowding out potentially dangerous bacteria and preventing them from sparking infections.

Antibiotics are bacteria hunters. They are on a search-and-destroy mission against the bugs within your body. But the drugs can't be made so specific that they only wipe out harmful bacteria. When an antibiotic enters your large intestine and is circulated through the blood stream, it destroys some of the friendly bugs that overwhelm harmful bacteria. Bad bugs then seize the opportunity and grow much more easily. Antibiotics can also kill bacteria that contribute to food digestion or make vitamins K and B.

If you have to take a course of antibiotics, doctors recommend that you eat plenty of natural yoghurt to replenish the stock of friendly bacteria. The best way to keep your good bugs alive, experts agree, is to only take antibiotics when you absolutely need them.

TOO MANY BUGS, TOO MANY DRUGS

The world is suffering from a craving for antibiotics. Around the globe, people have become reliant on the miracle drugs to cure everything from strep throats to stomach aches. Each year, doctors write more than 200 million prescriptions for antibiotics. In many developing countries, antibiotics such as penicillin are widely available without a doctor's consent, leading to more overuse. In Mongolia, for example, more than 40 per cent of children are given antibiotics without prescription for respiratory tract infections even though antibiotics do not work against them!

Lives put at risk

Used wisely, antibiotics offer an effective defence against many diseases. But the overuse of antibiotics can become a vicious cycle. Patients may think that an antibiotic such as amoxicillin cured their respiratory tract infection. But those infections are caused by viruses – not bacteria. Antibiotics are useless against viruses. The patients became better simply because the illness ran its course. But it is hard to convince them of that.

Pharmacists readily dispense antibiotics without prescription in the developing world because their income depends on drug sales. Pharmaceutical companies promote sales of antibiotics whether the patient needs them or not. Mothers look to any medication to make their children feel better quickly. The drugs are easy to abuse since people will rarely see harmful side effects for taking them incorrectly.

Prescription fever!

The more antibiotics are prescribed, the more chance bacteria will mutate and become drug-resistant. People who might have been cured easily just a few years ago have an increased chance of having their lives put at risk.

Imagine you wake up for school one morning with a runny nose and sore throat. Your head is woozy and you can barely stand.

It looks like you have a cold and will have to stay at home. If you go to the doctor, you may be given a prescription for an antibiotic. However, the next time this happens, stop and ask your doctor, "Do I really need an antibiotic?" and "Will it help me get well?" Increasingly, the answer is no and no.

Antibiotics can be extremely effective in killing bacteria. However, common ailments such as colds are not caused by bacteria. They are the result of a virus, infectious bugs that are similar to bacteria.

■ Antibiotics won't cure the common cold. They won't even help you feel better. Antibiotics only work against bacteria. Most colds are caused by viruses.

Like bacteria, viruses can multiply inside your healthy cells. They can also make you very sick. Most bronchitis, colds, laryngitis, and croup are caused by viruses.

Antibiotics do not work on viruses. It may take up to three weeks for a virus to clear up. Taking an antibiotic will not speed up the healing process. Inappropriate and overuse of antibiotics is widely credited with helping create superbugs.

When patients take drugs they do not need, super-resistant bugs can mutate to pass their genes on to other bacteria. Up to 75 per cent of antibiotics are used to treat upper respiratory or lung infections. Apart from pneumonia, most lung infections are caused by viruses, and antibiotics are useless against viruses!

Why do doctors prescribe drugs when they are not needed? Most doctors say they are influenced by the demands of their patients. Parents often demand a medicine to make their children feel better quickly. Physicians say it takes longer for them to explain why an antibiotic is a bad idea than to simply prescribe one. However, the Health Protection Agency makes clear that, in general, bugs do not need drugs.

About two-thirds of all antibiotics worldwide are obtained without a prescription and are inappropriately used against diseases such as TB, malaria, pneumonia, and routine child ailments such as ear infections.

In China and India, as well as some countries in Africa and Central and South America, antibiotic sales have soared. The **World Health Organization** says more than 50 per cent of those antibiotics are prescribed, dispensed, or sold inappropriately. And half of all patients fail to take medicines correctly.

VIRUSES VS BACTERIA

- Viruses are 10 to 100 times smaller than bacteria. If a virus were the size of, say, an average adult man, a bacterium would be the size of a dinosaur – over ten storeys tall!
- Viruses must have a living host, such as a plant or animal, to multiply. Most bacteria can grow on non-living surfaces.
- Viruses are intracellular organisms. That means they live inside a host cell. Viruses change the host cell's genetic material from its normal function so that the cell produces the virus itself. Most bacteria can multiply without the aid of the host cell.
- Antibacterial antibiotics can kill bacteria. Antibiotics cannot kill viruses. If you have a bacterial infection such as strep throat, you need an antibiotic. If you have a viral infection such as a cold, antibiotics cannot help you.

FIVE WAYS TO TELL IF YOU REALLY NEED AN ANTIBIOTIC

- Fever – If you have a fever, shivers, and chills, you could have a bacterial infection. But these are also common signs of viral illnesses such as colds. If a flu epidemic is running through your school, antibiotics called antivirals may be prescribed.

- The long run – Viral infections that hang around for a few weeks can sometimes turn into a bigger problem, like a bacterial bug. If your symptoms do not go away in two to three weeks, you might be prescribed an antibiotic, just to keep you from developing a nasty bug.

- The colour of ... achoo! – Nasal secretions tend to be thin and clear during a viral infection. Green or yellow mucus can be a sign of bacteria. However, some viral infections have a greenish discharge, too.

- Say ahh! – If a doctor looks down your sore throat and sees white spots, they are a good indicator of a bacterial infection, such as strep throat. Most colds start with a sore throat and move on to other symptoms, such as a runny nose. But if you have no other symptoms to go with your aching throat, it could be strep, which would call for an antibiotic. A doctor might take a culture – swabbing your throat for samples to grow in a lab and test – just to be sure.

- Testing, testing, 1, 2, 3 ... – A laboratory test is the only certain way to determine if you truly need an antibiotic. A physician can collect a sample of phlegm when you cough or blow your nose – or take a throat swab. Usually, growing and testing a culture can take a day or two. Doctors sometimes sidestep the expense and time of a lab test by making a decision based on your symptoms.

CASE STUDY

Two boys fighting two infections

It was just a cold. Nothing more was more bothering two-year-old Dalton Canterbury in 1999, according to his doctors in Pennsylvania, USA. But when Susan Canterbury woke her son from his afternoon nap, Dalton was so weak that he could barely hold his head up to eat.

Susan raced her son to the hospital in a panic. A **spinal tap** revealed that the boy had bacterial meningitis, a potentially life-threatening inflammation of the membranes around the brain and spinal cord. A test showed that Dalton's meningitis was caused by *Pneumococcus*. The bug was a well-known factor for ear infections in children. *Pneumococcus* was once considered easy and cheap to treat, but the bug had grown resistant to drugs such as penicillin. It had mutated into a killer superbug. Resistant bugs can be spread through nasal fluid, food, and saliva. Doctors believe that this is how the bug infected Dalton.

Doctors resorted to a powerful antibiotic that might kill the bug – if it was not too late. Doctors were worried that the infection had already invaded the part of Dalton's brain that controls sight. For weeks after Dalton left the hospital, his parents wondered if their child was blind for life.

For many years, resistant infections like the *Pneumococcus* that attacked Dalton were thought to be confined to hospital wards. But as the killer bugs multiply and become stronger, experts have been shocked at their ability to infect the outside community.

In 2004, 15-month-old Simon Macario began to show fairly typical health problems for a child his age: dehydration, ear and throat infections, asthma and allergy symptoms. Doctors prescribed antibiotics. Simon seemed to be responding, until he woke one night screaming, with a high fever. Simon was suffering from a strong infection. No matter what doctors tried, from **intravenous** antibiotics to the help of a heart–lung machine, Simon did not get any better.

Just days after Simon entered the hospital, his parents took him off his life-support machine. Two months later, an autopsy confirmed that Simon had died from methicillin-resistant *Staphylococcus aureus*, the staph infection known as MRSA. Staph infections were once easily treated with antibiotics. But as the strain became stronger and more resistant to drugs, MRSA has increasingly attacked healthy people in their homes.

Dalton was luckier. Months after leaving hospital, the toddler regained much of his eyesight, although he continued to face vision and learning problems. "You hear about people using antibiotics too often, but I don't think I ever realized the seriousness of this until Dalton got sick," his mother told the magazine *US News & World Report.* "I didn't know that we have overmedicated ourselves to the point that we've put ourselves in jeopardy."

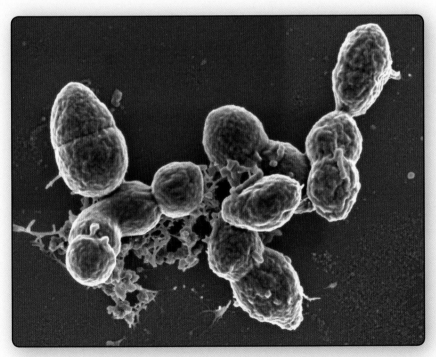

■ *Pneumococcus*, the bug that causes most ear infections, was once easy to treat with antibiotics like penicillin. But the bacteria has become drug resistant. Today, it can be a killer superbug, spreading through nasal fluid, food, and saliva.

WASH AWAY BUGS

What are we to do? Superbugs have overcome the world's most sophisticated medicines. Decades of research have failed to slow their invasion of our bodies. Is there any way to beat such a persistent enemy?

Hand-washing is the single most important way to stop the spread of many diseases, even superbugs. Good hand-washing habits may prevent more infections than the strongest antibiotic.

Dirty hands spread 80 per cent of the most common bacterial illnesses. One hand can be host to as many as 200 million organisms, including bacteria, viruses, and fungi. Most of the organisms on your skin are good bacteria. They crowd out bad bacteria and viruses. But dangerous germs can live on your hands for a short time. They can enter your body through one touch on a mucus membrane, such as the one in your mouth, nose, or eyes.

You may think you know how to wash your hands. But you are still getting sick. Chances are, you may not be washing at the right time or in the right way. No matter how old you are, you can always use a helping hand — or at least some hand-washing tips:

- Use soap and warm water. Water alone does not get rid of germs.
- Rub your hands together for no less than 20 seconds. Pay special attention to the fingertips and under the fingernails. That is where 95 per cent of germs are found.
- Rinse your hands for 10 seconds and dry them completely with a clean, dry towel if possible.

Be extra vigilant to wash your hands in these cases:

- Before meals
- Before and after preparing food, especially raw meat, poultry, or fish
- After using the toilet or after changing a child's nappy
- After blowing your nose, coughing, or sneezing
- Before and after being with someone who is sick
- Before inserting or removing contact lenses
- After playing with toys that might have been shared with other children
- After handling animals or pets or picking up their droppings

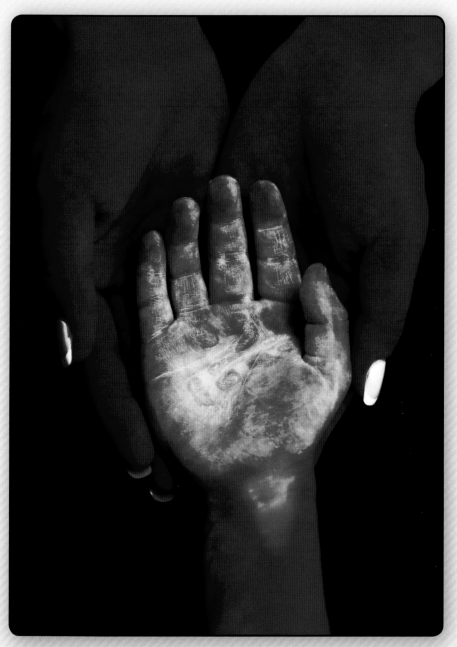

The child's hand in this photograph had a special fluid applied to it and then the hand was washed. The fluid shows up under a special light to reveal areas that have not been washed effectively (light areas). This shows the importance of thorough hand washing to remove bacteria and prevent the harmful effects of cross-contamination.

Ear today – trouble tomorrow?

To treat or not to treat? When it comes to ear infections, that is the question. However, for doctors, parents, young children, maybe even the health of everyone, there is no clear answer.

Ear infections can be terribly painful. They are a common and often recurring ailment for infants and toddlers. They can be excruciating for sick children who wake up screaming in the night and heart-breaking for parents who take care of them. Thousands of children go to the doctor with ear infections each year. No wonder so many of them leave with antibiotics. In fact, ear infections are the main reason children are given prescriptions. But some experts are delivering a diagnosis that will shock parents: many of those children may not have needed the drugs.

There is little consensus over how to treat ear infections in children. Some doctors push for administering antibiotics. Others have a hands-off approach. Many studies have shown that as many as 80 per cent of ear infections get better on their own without the aid of antibiotics. And their overuse can encourage the growth of drug-resistant superbugs.

Most experts agree that antibiotics will not cure an ear infection any faster than letting it run its course. However, many think that the drugs may prevent relapses and halt the infection before it gets worse. The problem, physicians say, is that true bacterial ear infections are hard to diagnose. If a doctor clearly sees a red bulge in the ear, it is a strong sign of a middle-ear infection. The bulge is most likely caused by pus from a bacterial infection that needs antibiotic treatment.

WHAT DO YOU THINK?

If you have ever had an ear infection, you know how much they hurt. You want fast relief. But now that you know many ear infections will clear up on their own within three days, would you still ask a doctor for an antibiotic? Or would you be willing to let it run its course?

■ Ear infections don't always require an antibiotic. Some studies show that as many as 80 per cent of ear infections get better on their own without antibiotics.

Critics say that many children are prescribed antibiotics before doctors can confirm that they have an actual infection. And they are increasingly being given super-powerful antibiotics for a relatively mild condition. Why? Many physicians explain that they do not want to take chances with young patients and watch their ear get worse. Others are responding to desperate parents' requests for immediate help. Not only are mums and dads anxious to relieve their children's agonizing pain, but most childcare centres will not allow children who are ill to come to nursery. Likewise, parents often have trouble scheduling a second doctor visit if their child's ear infection does not improve on its own.

Today, in cases where a severe ear infection is not 100 per cent confirmed, many physicians are trying a modified route dubbed SNAP: Safety Net Antibiotic Prescription. Doctors can write a drug prescription for a child, but ask the parents to wait before filling it. If the child gets better within three days, no antibiotic is needed.

CASE STUDY

C. diff

A superbug spread through UK hospital wards, taking victim after victim. In all, the bug would be linked to more than 300 deaths, each seemingly worse than the last. A healthy 86-year-old woman who worked part-time in a clothes shop was admitted for an eye infection, only to find herself suffering through agonizing chronic diarrhoea. An 87-year-old World War II veteran wasted away in such pain that he pleaded with his daughter to let him die. A 77-year-old woman caught the fatal infection after a blood transfusion. Her family was unaware of the cause of death until they saw it on her death certificate: *Clostridium difficile*. It is also known as *C. difficile* or C. diff.

Until recently, C. diff was thought to be harmless and friendly bacteria, a normal part of the digestive system. But, in 2005 and 2006, another side to C. diff appeared. In a scandal that shook the UK medical community, three English hospitals managed by a National Health Service trust were investigated for shockingly poor sanitary conditions. Reports by the BBC and UK newspapers, including the *Guardian* and *The Times*, blamed cost cuts, nursing shortages, and gross executive negligence.

The hospitals set the scene for the C. diff outbreak. And the very antibiotics that were meant to save lives played a part in taking them.

Who is to blame for the deaths? Certainly the unsanitary conditions at the understaffed, overcrowded hospitals were disgusting. Staff members were frequently spotted moving from patient to patient without washing their hands. Worse, C. diff often causes severe diarrhoea. News services reported that some patients were told to relieve themselves in their beds when nurses did not have time to take them to the toilet. Others were left to lie for hours on soiled mattresses.

However, look closer and you will find another cause for the rash of C. diff deaths: antibiotics.

In the late 1970s, researchers recognized that the seemingly harmless C. diff bug could cause diseases under the right circumstances. The unhealthy conditions at the hospital certainly allowed C. diff to flourish, a 2007 report by the British Care Quality Commission concluded. But antibiotic-resistance among bacteria is also to blame. C. diff is not just resistant to antibiotics, it thrives on them.

"Someone has to be held accountable for these deaths ... these patients didn't die by chance. They died because they contracted C. diff ... because of poor hygiene and care."

Son of one of the victims, reported in the *Guardian*

You may have C. diff in your intestines. C. diff makes **spores** that can even spread through the air. Once C. diff settles on your hands, it can easily travel through your mouth to your gut. But when you are healthy, and not taking antibiotics, the millions of good bacteria in your system keep the C. diff under control. C. diff usually attacks elderly patients in hospitals or nursing homes. Most of these people are being treated with antibiotics for unrelated infections. The antibiotics do not target the C. diff. They shrink the levels of good bacteria to tiny amounts while the C. diff multiply at a rapid rate, overpopulating your intestine or colon. With the balance of good bacteria and bad bacteria thrown off kilter, C. diff sparks diarrhoea and other illnesses which can quickly become serious.

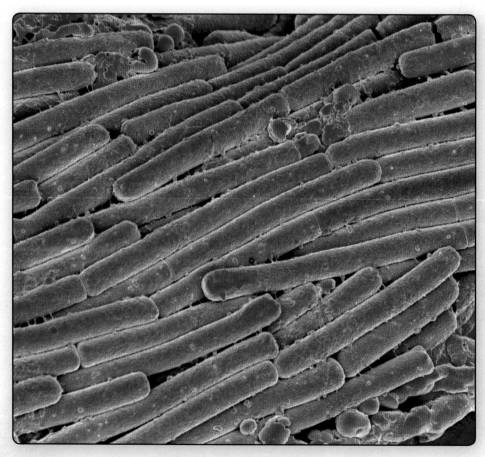

■ C. diff spores can withstand heat, disinfectants, and alcohol. The best way to lower the risk of C. diff infections in hospitals is by following strict infection control policies.

"You wash your hands, you wash the beds after the patients have been there, you have the laundry services working and everything should be okay."

Mark Enright, a specialist in hospital-acquired infections at London's Imperial College, reported in *The Times*

The mighty C. diff spores can withstand heat, disinfectants, and even alcohol. Still, experts say the best way to lower the risk of C. diff is for hospitals to maintain vigorous infection control policies. A healthcare commission called for hospitals to closely monitor infections, maintain "effective" hygiene levels, and ensure that antibiotic prescriptions are appropriate. Just as crucially, staff must pay attention to the smallest details.

Recently, the healthcare commission concluded that at least 90 deaths were directly tied to the infection, with more than 200 others having some link to C. diff. Hospital officials resigned, although no criminal charges were pressed. In 2009, the same commission praised the hospitals' improvements, which included better standards of cleaning and infection control in areas such as hand hygiene.

However, while hospitals have initiated tougher hygiene policies, C. diff has proven hard to kill. As UK hospitals continue to see C. diff cases, US healthcare facilities are also reporting as many as half a million C. diff infections a year, with 15,000 to 20,000 deaths. C. diff now rivals MRSA as one of the top superbug threats. Like MRSA, C. diff is spreading into the general community. Over 40 per cent of new C. diff infections cases occur outside hospitals.

Anti-soaps overkill

Today, many homes and schools use **antibacterial** soap to keep hands clean and surfaces sterile. But increasingly, experts say antibacterial products such as hand cleansers and detergents do more harm than good. Experts say they are no more effective at keeping you bug-free than soap and water. And antibacterials contain chemicals that stay on surfaces longer then soap and water. That means they continue killing bacteria at a low rate. That drives bacteria to become even more resistant. There are legitimate uses for antibacterial products in healthcare settings. But, at home, nothing beats soap and water.

Watch out for changing rooms

Be especially careful about hygiene in moist, sweaty places such as gyms and changing rooms. Bugs such as MRSA thrive in cramped, crowded places. They have flared up everywhere, from daycare centres to prisons. In changing rooms, make sure not to share personal items such as towels or razors. Always wear shower shoes or flip-flops. Wipe down surfaces such as benches or toilet seats.

Antibacterial soap is popular in schools and homes, but some say it is no more effective than soap and water. Worse, it may help bugs become drug-resistant.

Keep it to yourself

Even outside of changing rooms, do not share personal items. You know better than to let a friend borrow a toothbrush. But how about a hair brush? You can pass bacteria on through any number of items. Mobile phones, for example, can sometimes carry staph bacteria.

Hospital hygiene

Many superbugs have their origins in hospitals. That is where MRSA made its first appearance. That is where most C. diff infections lurk. Whether you are making a quick trip to an Accident and Emergency department or you are having a prolonged stay in the surgical ward, be mindful of hospital infections. Don't be shy. Ask your doctor about the facility's infection rates. They should be able to give you figures on their hand-hygiene compliance. And it is your right to sound an alarm if you see something suspicious, such as a healthcare worker touching a bed pan before they touch you. Hospital staff should always wash or use hand gel directly before they put their hands on you. If you do not feel comfortable speaking your mind, or you are worried you will miss something, make sure you bring a parent or friend. Give them strict instructions to watch out for signs of trouble. Remember, superbugs never sleep!

Smart drugs

You have a part to play in fighting superbugs. The best thing you can do is be responsible about antibiotic use. Firstly, do not demand antibiotics from your doctor. Before he or she prescribes a drug, ask if it is really necessary or if your symptoms will clear up on their own. Secondly, if you do need an antibiotic, make sure you take the entire amount prescribed. About two-thirds of people simply stop taking their medicine when they start feeling better. But unless you finish an entire prescription, there is a good chance you have only killed the weakest bugs and left the hardest-to-kill bacteria alive inside you. Those partly resistant drugs can multiply and grow stronger. Finally, never take someone else's antibiotic. It may not be the right medicine for your illness. And it could end up killing your body's good bacteria.

ANIMAL FARM

In 1983, eighteen people in four Midwestern states in the United States had developed bad cases of **Salmonella**. They were showing all the common symptoms: nausea, vomiting, diarrhoea. One of the elderly victims even died of dehydration. Like other cases of food poisoning, the patients had a link. They had all eaten hamburgers from the same beef source.

Fear of food?

This was not a straightforward case. Doctors tried to treat patients with a series of antibiotics, the normal routine for *Salmonella* poisoning. But one after another, each drug failed to defeat the food bug, which had now mutated into a superbug.

This time, however, the superbug outbreak may not have started in people. The cattle herd that produced the contaminated beef had been fed antibiotics. Like humans, the cows reacted to antibiotics by harbouring drug-resistant bacteria. These *Salmonella* superbugs may have been passed on from slaughtered cattle that were made into hamburgers.

All foods contain some form of bacteria. Most are not harmful. Some of them are part of our everyday lives, such as in the cheese and yogurt we eat. But there are some harmful food-borne bugs, notably *Salmonella* and *E. coli*. You cannot always tell if your food is harmful just by looking at it, or even by tasting it. *Salmonella* may not make food appear, smell, or even taste off. But it can make people very sick with abdominal cramps, diarrhoea, nausea and vomiting.

Most cases of food-borne illness are not reported. That makes it hard for scientists to determine how many people around the world are affected by bad food bacteria. Experts believe that between 696,000 and 3.8 million people contract *Salmonella* poisoning each year. In the United States, about 40,000 *Salmonella* illness are reported annually. However, many milder cases are not diagnosed, so the actual number of infections may be thirty or more times higher. Young children, the elderly, and people with immune system problems are most at risk from *Salmonella,* and about 400 people die from it each year.

Food bugs such as *Salmonella* and *E. coli* are often spread from meat that is not properly cooked. And it is not always possible to tell if a burger is fine just by looking at it or even tasting it.

France closely monitors food-borne illnesses and reports 8,000 cases of *Salmonella* poisoning each year, with 553 deaths. In Australia, there are an estimated 5.4 million cases of food-borne illness every year, causing 120 deaths.

According to the World Health Organization, each year over 22 million people worldwide are infected with typhoid fever, a deadly form of *Salmonella* infection. It kills 216,000 victims annually.

Food bugs are generally spread from meat that is not cooked properly. You can also get them from drinking raw milk and **unpasteurized** apple juice or cider. Some, such as *E. coli*, can be passed from person to person through hand contact or by touching surfaces such as kitchen counters and cutting boards. Washing carefully can prevent infection.

Food bugs, particularly *Salmonella*, are becoming more and more drug-resistant. Antibiotics that once helped with the symptoms of *Salmonella* infection do not work as well as they used to. While some cases may be explained by people overdoing their antibiotic dose, others are asking different questions, such as "Why are animals being given antibiotics?," and "Can their effects be passed on to humans?" The answer does not lie in a laboratory. To solve this problem, you have to visit a farm.

African outbreak

Around the world, *Salmonella* poisoning is a way of life. *Salmonella* outbreaks can be uncomfortable but experts have always believed they are rarely fatal in large numbers. Disturbingly, that line of thinking may have changed due to a powerful new drug-resistant strain of *Salmonella* bacteria that has emerged in Africa over the last decade.

The bug, *Salmonella enterica* Typhimurium, is usually spread through food. It causes diarrhoea and is usually not fatal. However, a new strain called ST313 kills 1 in 4 infected people, mostly children and vulnerable adults (those with weak immune systems due to, for example, AIDS or malnutrition). It has been found in West, East, and Central Africa. A collaboration of African and UK scientists have discovered that ST313 can mutate to become resistant to many commonly used antibiotics.

One researcher, Robert Heyderman, director of the Malawi-Liverpool-Wellcome Trust Research Programme, believes the bacteria can be passed from human to human without passing through animals or food.

"*Salmonella* is a bacteria which we know is passed on to humans from eggs, meat or milk, but we think this bacteria could be coming off cutlery and crockery. It is in the home and everyone, especially small children, is vulnerable," he said.

Scientist are studying the new strain for clues on how to beat it. But that job is harder in the developing world, where most cases are not reported to healthcare officials. Experts say that, outside of the most developed African countries such as South Africa, no one knows how many people have been infected with ST313 and how many people have died.

Mystery meat

Livestock and poultry are farmed, go to slaughterhouses, and end up in the supermarket. You see the finished products, the tightly wrapped raw beef and chicken legs. But few people actually get to see the animals before they are processed.

Today, most animals bred for slaughter are crammed into tight quarters. Their diets are strictly scrutinized. Farmers say there is no other way to manage huge livestock herds in limited spaces.

But these tightly packed animals are not just fed grass and grain. They are given lots and lots of antibiotics. Feeding animals huge doses of antibiotic drugs just before they are slaughtered is one of the most controversial practices in the food industry. In 2009 in the United States, 14,500 tonnes of antibiotics were sold for use in animal agriculture.

Why do animals need antibiotics? One reason is that they live in such close quarters that they can easily infect each other with diseases. Farmers give drugs to healthy animals to prevent bacterial bugs spreading disease through the herd.

Farm animals are often fed antibiotics to keep them from infecting each other in close quarters and to promote their growth.

Even more controversially, animals are given antibiotics to increase their growth. Scientists are not sure how antibiotics in feed and water help fatten animals. But farmers use them because bigger animals produce more meat for supermarket shelves.

The World Health Organization estimates that 50 per cent of all antibiotics produced around the world are used in farm animals. In the United States, that number may be as high as 70 per cent. The **Union of Concerned Scientists** estimates that 70 per cent of those are used simply to promote animal growth, not to treat or prevent illness. Increasingly, "free range" farmers are raising animals without the use of antibiotics for growth. But their numbers comprise just a fraction of the food industry.

Dosing animals, critics contend, has the same effect as overusing antibiotics on humans. The bugs become resistant to the drugs. Pigs and cows that become food are breeding grounds for resistant bacteria. A 2006 report by the European Food Safety Authority found that more than 50 per cent of poultry farms in some **European Union** countries were contaminated with *Salmonella*, leading to worries about egg safety. About 62 per cent of farms in the Czech Republic were contaminated, along with 55 per cent in Poland and 51 per cent in Spain. The United Kingdom ranked third lowest in Europe, with just under 12 per cent *Salmonella* contamination.

Can animals pass their antibiotic-resistant superbugs to humans? That is still a hot debate. Not many studies conclusively link drug-fed animals to superbugs in humans. But it is possible. Scientists have seen antibiotic-resistant strains of food-borne bugs such as *Salmonella*. And there are sporadic reports of people being infected with these bugs, presumably through food.

Many nations have decided to take action. Europe has restricted the use of antibiotics in animals for a decade. In 2006, the European Union banned all antibiotics for animal growth. The World Health Organization recommended stopping the use of antibiotics as growth promoters in animal feeds.

Critics say the United States has lagged behind in preventing a crisis. In 2005, the US Food and Drug Administration banned drugs called fluoroquinolones that were widely used in poultry farming. Fluoroquinolones were linked to a drug-resistant infection in humans. It took five years to remove it from farms. Experts say this was mostly due to challenges from the food animal and pharmaceutical industries.

Read the arguments for each side.

YES – Antibiotics in animals *should* be banned

- Seventy per cent of all the antibiotic drugs produced in the world are given to healthy herds, just to prevent them from getting diseases in cramped pens and to make them grow bigger more quickly to produce more meat.

- Super-strong strains of food-borne bacteria, mutations of *Salmonella* and *E. coli*, have been detected in feed animals.

- There is increasing evidence that humans can be infected by the resistant bacteria by eating contaminated meat, by being in close contact with infected animals, or through bacteria spores in the environment.

- By 2006, the European Union had wiped out all antibiotic use in farm animals. Some studies have shown that bans on antibiotics in Europe have coincided with decreasing rates of superbug infections in humans

NO – Antibiotics in animals *should not* be banned

- Animals in close quarters can pass bacteria between each other. It is important that these animals get antibiotics before they become sick and spread disease to the rest of the herd.

- There is a greater risk of sick animals transmitting illnesses to people than a drug-resistant bacteria jumping from an animal to a human.

- There are no studies that establish a direct link between antibiotic use in farm animals and deadly drug-resistant infections in people. There is no conclusive evidence that a superbug can travel – through food, by touch, or in the air – between livestock and humans.

- Making cattle grow bigger helps the world's food industry and the global economy. Animals fed antibiotics grow faster and provide more meat. This provides more food for people, more jobs, and lower prices around the world.

What do you think?

Protect yourself – don't be afraid of your dinner

Are there nasty bacteria lurking in your burger? Is there a superbug in your salad?

Many food-borne bugs are spread through undercooked meat. *Salmonella* and *E. coli* can also appear in raw milk, unpasteurized apple juice, or water that is not purified with chlorine. You are unlikely to have those drinks in your fridge, but check the use-by date on labels. Very rarely, food bacteria can appear in leafy vegetables. Here's how you can protect yourself:

- Wash, wash, wash – Proper hand hygiene can eliminate almost half of all food-borne illnesses. Always wash your hands thoroughly before and after: handling food, eating, going to the toilet, changing a baby's nappy, touching raw food, touching an animal, sneezing or coughing, handling rubbish, using the phone or touching your face, hair, or an open cut or sore.

- Do not cross-contaminate – When raw meat comes in contact with other foods, cross-contamination occurs. For example, when you handle raw meat on a cutting board and then chop lettuce for a salad without washing the board, bacteria from the meat contaminates the lettuce. Do not use the same utensils for meat and other foods. If you use a fork to put raw meat in the oven, use a clean spatula to remove the cooked meat. Do not forget to wipe down countertops and cutting boards. Store raw meat on the bottom shelf of the refrigerator so it does not drip on other food.

- Keep hot foods hot – Harmful bacteria are destroyed by cooking food properly. Only eat foods that are properly cooked. If you cut into chicken and it looks pink and raw inside, do not eat it. The colour and texture of meat does not prove that it is well cooked. Use a food thermometer to check the temperature.

- Keep cold foods cold – Cover and refrigerate food right away. Bacteria can grow in foods that sit at room temperature. Meat, fish, milk, and eggs should be kept cold. Do not defrost your food at room temperature. Thaw it in the fridge overnight, under cold running water, or in the microwave.

- Are fruits and vegetables safe? – Do not avoid fruits and vegetables. They are still among the best foods you can eat. However, *Salmonella* and *E. coli* have spread through leafy foods such as spinach and lettuce. Before you eat salad, wash it thoroughly. Keep in mind that washing may not remove all contaminations. If there is a food poisoning outbreak, check TV, radio, and newspaper reports for advice on which foods to avoid. In 2010, in the United Kingdom, about 140 cases of *Salmonella*, including one death, were linked to a batch of bad bean sprouts.

STILL NOT SURE? TIME AND TEMPERATURE ARE THE KEY

How do you know when food is OK to eat or when it should be thrown away?

Imagine a summer barbecue. After everyone has finished eating, there is a plate of leftover burgers and chicken. How long before you have to throw them away? If it is a very hot day (30 degrees Celsius – 86 degrees Fahenheit – or higher) it can stay out for about one hour. On a cooler day, it may be left up to two hours. But do not eat it after that, even if it still looks all right. If you want to save cooked meat for leftovers, refrigerate it straight away, before it goes bad.

How long can leftovers stay in the fridge before they go off? It depends on the food, but it is best to eat them within three to four days.

NEW HORIZONS

Not so long ago, doctors would not have been as gravely concerned over patients like Dalton Canterbury or Bo Salisbury. By the mid-1960s, there were plenty of antibiotics in the world – as many as 25,000 different products. Many more were being discovered in laboratories. If one drug did not cure a bacterial infection, another would. And if none of them worked, it would not be too long before science developed one that did.

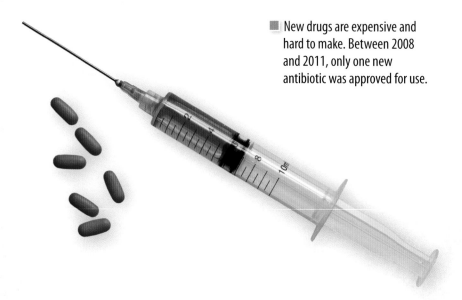

New drugs are expensive and hard to make. Between 2008 and 2011, only one new antibiotic was approved for use.

But times have changed. Superbugs have grown faster and stronger. Most experts agree that science and drug producers have not kept up. New antibiotics are being developed more slowly now than at any time in their history. Just one new antibiotic has been approved for use in the last three years. Many companies have stopped developing antibiotics altogether. Only five major pharmaceutical companies still had active antibacterial discovery programmes in 2008. And only a few compounds have been identified that even have the potential to become effective new antibiotics. According to a 2008 study, of 167 antibodies under development around the world, only 15 showed promise in battling bugs that are resistant to many drugs.

Help on the way?

Most antibiotics that are still being developed remain in the very early phases of research. What happened? Why did antibiotics research flourish in the 1940s and '50s but fizzle out in the 2000s? Some claim science became complacent. They turned their attention to other problems such as viral infections even though resistance to common antibiotics grew.

For drug companies, developing antibiotics offers more risks than profits. They are expensive to create, costing hundreds of millions of pounds and taking as long as 10 years to bring to market.

Even if companies find new antibiotics, the drugs may not be profitable for them. Pharmaceutical companies make money on drugs that are used repeatedly, every day, for chronic diseases such as heart problems or depression. Antibiotics, by their very nature, are meant to be used sparingly. You take them for a week or two, then stop. That routine may make good clinical sense. But it does not make large profits.

While big pharmaceutical giants focus on profitable drugs, small firms have trouble funding any drug development at all. For example, one company may put all its effort into an acid reflux medicine rather than produce drugs that fight an array of bacteria.

In the United States, many say the government-run drug approval process is too long, costly, and overcautious. The federal Food and Drug Administration (FDA) tests and approves medicine. Drug firms complain that the FDA is slow and orders too many tests. Others say the FDA is safeguarding public health.

In the United Kingdom and Sweden, governments have teamed up with drug companies to share the costs and risks of creating new drugs. The goal, as Swedish health officials explained in the *British Medical Journal,* is "delinking research and development costs from drug pricing and the return that drug companies receive on investment". If companies do not have to worry about recouping production costs with sales, they are more likely to take a chance on experimental drugs or new antibiotics.

Not everybody agrees that incentives will work. Some worry that drug companies still will not focus on drugs for serious bacterial diseases.

Some fear that profit-seeking firms will work on medications for less serious but more common problems, such as ear infections. The more common the disease, the more profit can be made from marketing the drugs, even for conditions that will clear up on their own.

New antibiotics are not easy to make. Most antibiotics are created from natural sources such as bacteria and fungi. Others are synthetics produced in labs. But almost as soon as a drug is created, superbugs learn to resist them.

Penicillin was the first antibiotic, the "miracle drug" that saved thousands of lives. When superbugs outwitted penicillin, a new drug, methicillin, was meant to replace it. But by 1990, most staph strains were resistant to methicillin. Doctors tried Vancomycin. They had never expected to use Vancomycin on a wide scale. It was the only known antibiotic left that was still effective against certain life-threatening infections.

WHAT DO YOU THINK?

One way to spot superbugs in healthcare is to screen hospital patients for bacteria. But who should be screened? Some think that every patient should undergo screening, even if they are admitted for something as seemingly small as a broken arm. Others say that is not reasonable. It is impossible for understaffed hospitals to screen every patient. And patients should have the right to refuse tests, especially when they are unrelated to the reason for their hospital stay.

The 2006 death of Maribel Espaba, the young British nurse who contracted a fatal MRSA-related pneumonia just five days after giving birth to her first child, changed the way the health authorities looked at bacterial infections. Spurred by a public outcry, mandatory superbug screening for all surgical patients was introduced.

Each of the 12 million people who undergo planned operations in UK hospitals now receive quick screen tests, swabs from their nose, another under their armpit, and an occasional third from the groin. The test results are finalized within a day or two.

What do you think? Should all patients be screened? Should it only be for surgical patients? How would you decide?

That was until the late 1990s, when the first known Vancomycin-resistant bug appeared in a Tokyo hospital. A year later, the same infections invaded hospitals in Michigan and New Jersey in the United States. Today, Vancomycin-resistant bacteria are not epidemics, they are pandemic. That means they are now common, particularly in hospitals and nursing homes all over the world.

Drugs that have followed, such as quinupristin and linezolid, each cost about $400 million and took more than a decade to develop. But superbugs could resist them almost by the time they were first used in healthcare settings.

As resistant bacteria grow, scientists are in a desperate race to discover new agents that can finally trick the superbugs, before it is too late.

There is continuing research to find drugs that can contend with superbugs but it is slow and painstaking work and not always profitable.

CASE STUDY

The battlefield superbug

On 10 July 2008, Marine Corporal Sean Locker was guarding a military convoy in Iraq when an explosion blasted him off the ground. A suicide bomber had blown up a nearby car. Shrapnel ripped across Locker's face, instantly blinding him. His lung collapsed. His left arm was shredded. Locker told *Forbes* magazine that he knew it would have to be amputated. "I tried to stay level-headed," he says.

Locker, 25, was flown to a hospital in Maryland, USA. While there, he faced another enemy, one that was striking more and more soldiers at war. It was a bacterial infection called *Acinetobacter*. After the operation, military doctors found the infection in Locker's amputation spot.

Doctors had seen soldiers with combat wounds succumbing to this virulent bug. Some had infections of the bone, bloodstream, or internal organs. Others had limbs that were so infected that doctors had no choice but to amputate them.

Acinetobacter has always been a difficult bug to treat. Now it was getting harder. Doctors found that the drug was not responding to normal antibiotics. This was a sure sign that *Acinetobacter* was a superbug.

A 2010 study found that *Acinetobacter* has quickly become stronger. In recent years, there has been a 300 per cent increase in the number of *Acinetobacter* cases that are resistant to antibiotics.

Physicians have always used three drugs to fight *Acinetobacter*. The most common, imipenem, can cause seizures. But the superbug had already mutated to resist imipenem. Another drug, amikacin, is ineffective against some strains of the bacteria. A third, colistin, is an old antibiotic. Doctors had to search for it among reserve supplies. The medical community has all but stopped using colistin because of its toxic effects on the kidneys.

Locker has recovered better than other soldiers. His infection seemed to react well to imipenem. He is in good health.

So far, few deaths are attributed to *Acinetobacter* infections. Most were among patients who suffered from serious health problems before they contracted the bacteria. But experts worry the bacteria are hiding on the battlefield. Many military healthcare facilities are screening soldiers for *Acinetobacter*. They are isolating contaminated patients away from those who are not infected.

"It is a scary thing ... you've only got three antibiotics, one so old that we had to bring it back from the archives," an infection-control expert told *Forbes*.

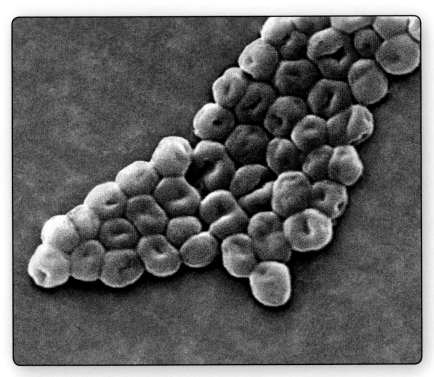

The deadly bacteria *Acinetobacter* has attacked soldiers on the battlefield. Some of their infections have been so bad that doctors have had to amputate their limbs.

New hope

Have we already lost the battle of the bugs? Is it time to surrender? Should we throw up our hands and admit that humankind is no match for microscopic microbes?

The answer is yes, and no. Scientists agree that we will never completely beat superbugs. We can never wipe out bacteria. We would not want to. They are an essential part of Earth, from our environment to our bodies. Friendly bacteria help us digest food, break down waste, and produce essential vitamins that our bodies need. In nature, friendly bacteria help recycle compost and even break up hazardous waste.

Bacteria are smart bugs. They have mutated to survive. And they will always find a way to resist whatever research throws at them. But that does not mean we cannot slow them down. From washing our hands to pursuing new drugs, there is a part to be played by every school child and scientist.

Researchers have not given up the quest for new antibiotics. Many are trying to discover microbes that superbugs have never seen before, searching in areas as remote as vast deserts, the Amazon, and the ocean floor. New antibiotics might be extracted from plants. Bacteria can infect plants as well as animals. Plants produce their own chemicals to keep bacteria under control. The rainforest plants, for example, are considered an excellent source of molecules that could produce new antibiotics.

The world must engage in serious debates about tough topics. Should antibiotics be used on farm animals? Can we curb the availability of over-the-counter antibiotics, dangerous drugs that can be bought in many countries without a prescription? Can the world band together to provide developing nations with clean drinking water and good sanitation, cutting down two major pathways for the growth of superbugs?

Activists have spread the word of "prudent prescribing", persuading doctors not to give antibiotics when they are not needed and asking patients not to insist that their doctor give them a tablet for every symptom.

There is also a lot that you can do. If you need an antibiotic, use all of it. About two-thirds of people stop taking their medicine when they start feeling better. But that means you have only wiped out the weaker bugs. The strongest bacteria are still lurking.

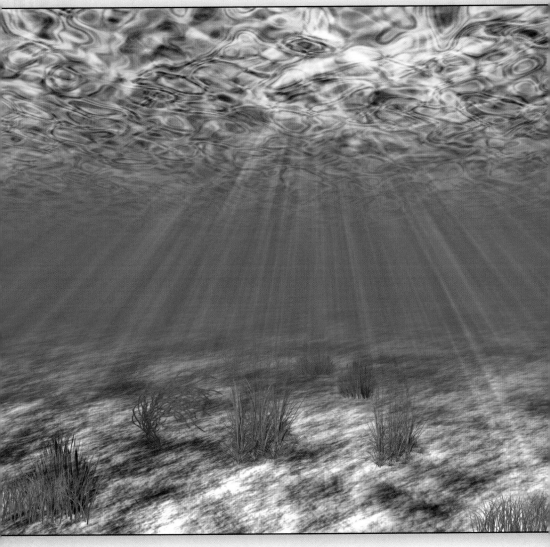

■ Where will we find the clues to the next generation of antibiotics? Scientists are searching everywhere, from the rainforests to the ocean floors.

Remember that antibacterial antibiotics only work against bacterial infections, such as strep throat. A third of people believe that antibiotics work against the common cold. But they do not. Colds are caused by viruses.

Most of all, you can practise good hygiene. Never share personal items such as toothbrushes and hair brushes. Be careful when you handle food. Science has spent decades and vast sums of money trying to defeat superbugs. But the most effective weapon in the war is probably in your bathroom: soap and water. Wash your hands and you are likely to win the battle of the bug.

WHAT HAVE WE LEARNED?

Are you ready to fight the superbugs? See how well you remember the facts and information you have read in this book. If you can pass this test, you might be a future Bug Beater.

Humans vs bugs

1 Microscopic, single-cell "bugs", the most abundant life forms on earth, are called:
   a) Genes
   b) Bacteria
   c) Viruses
   d) None of the above

Answer: b) Bacteria

2 The world's first antibiotic was:
   a) Penicillin
   b) Methicillin
   c) E. coli
   d) None of the above

Answer: a) Penicillin

3 True or false?
Not all bacteria are bad

Answer: True. "Good" bacteria fend off diseases. They make your immune system stronger, produce vitamins and even help you digest your food. Bacteria help keep our environment clean. They play an important role in recycling nutrients and converting toxic waste.

Inside Science

1 Today, what percentage of all bacteria are thought to be resistant to at least one antibiotic?
   a) 10
   b) 30
   c) 70
   d) None of the above

Answer: c) 70

2 Which of these is a method that superbugs use to overcome the affect of antibiotics?
   a) Mutating, or changing, their genetic make-up
   b) Passing their resistant genes to other bacteria
   c) Reproducing at incredibly rapid rates
   d) All of the above

Answer: d) All of the above

3 True or false?
The flesh-eating bacteria that cause necrotizing fasciitis can only enter a human body through your mouth or an open sore.

Answer: False. Necrotizing fasciitis enters your body through skin trauma. That can mean a cut or even a deep bruise.

Too many bugs, too many drugs

1 Which of these traits belong to viruses and which belong to bacteria?
   a) Must have a living host, a plant or animal, to multiply
   b) Live inside a host cell
   c) Some antibiotics are effective in killing them

Answer: Viruses: a) and b); bacteria: c)

2 Which of the following are most effective in keeping you safe from bad bacteria?
   a) Soap and water
   b) Antibacterial soap
   c) Sharing toothbrushes
   d) All of the above

Answer: a) Soap and water

3 True or false? Hand-washing is the single most important way to stop the spread of many diseases, even superbugs.

Answer: True. Dirty hands spread 80 per cent of the most common bacterial illnesses. One hand can be host to as many as 200 million organisms, including bacteria, viruses, and fungi.

Animal farm

1 Which of these would *not* be a source of *Salmonella* poisoning?
   a) Dried flowers
   b) Undercooked meat
   c) Unpasteurized apple juice

Answer: a) Dried flowers

2 True or false? Half of all antibiotics produced around the world are used in farm animals.

Answer: True. And an estimated 70 per cent of antibiotics used on animals are intended to promote animal growth, not to treat or prevent illness.

3 True or false? European nations have banned all antibiotics use in farm animals.

Answer: True. Since 2006, no European Union country can use antibiotics to promote farm animal growth. Some studies have shown that bans on antibiotics in Europe have coincided with decreasing rates of superbugs in humans.

New horizons

1 True or false? Just one new antibiotic has been approved for use in the last three years.

Answer: True. In fact, only five major pharmaceutical companies are even actively trying to develop new antibiotics.

2 In which of these locations are scientists searching for possible new microbes to be used in new antibiotics?
   a) Deserts
   b) The Amazon
   c) The ocean floor
   d) All of the above

Answer: d) All of the above

3 True or false? New antibiotics might be extracted from plants.

Answer: True. Bacteria can infect plants as well as animals. Plants produce their own chemicals to keep bacteria under control.

SUPERBUGS TIMELINE

1660	Dutch cloth merchant Antonie van Leeuwenhoek is the first to see bacteria. Looking at a sample of pond water through magnifying lenses, he discovers that one drop teems with tiny bacteria.
1870	German scientist/physician Robert Koch proves that bacteria cause some illnesses.
1928	Scottish researcher Alexander Fleming accidentally discovers penicillin when a fungus interacts with bacteria-filled Petri dishes. This discovery will lead to the first antibiotic and save millions of lives.
1943	Drug companies begin mass production of penicillin
1945	In a *New York Times* interview, Fleming warns that misusing his penicillin could lead to a mutant, medicine-resistant bacterial strain
1954	Nearly 1,000 tonnes of antibiotics are produced in the US. By 2000, that number will rise to nearly 23,000 tonnes.
1958	American geneticist Joshua Lederberg wins Nobel Prize for proving that bacteria can exchange genetic material among themselves and spread resistance
1960	A powerful new antibiotic, methicillin, is introduced in the UK
1961	The first methicillin-resistant infection, MRSA, appears in the UK
1963	MRSA appears in Denmark
1967	Penicillin-resistant *Streptococcus pneumoniae* is found among a tribe in New Guinea, the first widespread superbug outside of a hospital on record

1968	More than 12,000 people in Guatemala die from a diarrhoea epidemic. It is caused by a bug that is resistant to four different types of antibiotics.
1983	Eighteen people in the US are hit with drug-resistant *Salmonella* after eating beef from cows given antibiotics. Eleven are hospitalized and one dies.
1986	Sweden bans use of antibiotics to make farm animals grow faster
1992	Antibiotic-resistant bacterial infections kill a record 13,000 hospital patients worldwide. About 5 per cent of all bacteria tested in the US are resistant to penicillin
2003	Drug-resistant *Acinetobacter* infects Iraq war-wounded in military hospitals. By 2010, doctors will see a 300 per cent increase in antibiotic-resistant *Acinetobacter* cases, many among Iraq war soldiers.
2006	European Union bans use of antibiotics for farm animal growth
2007	Study finds 10 times as many MRSA cases in US hospitals as previously thought
2007	A report by the British Care Quality Commission links at least 90 deaths to an outbreak of the drug-resistant bacteria *C. difficile* in British hospitals during 2005–2006.
2008	A report shows that antibiotics in animal feed have contributed to a rise in antibiotic-resistant *E. coli, Salmonella,* and MRSA in people
2008	Only five major pharmaceutical companies have active antibacterial discovery programmes
2009	Fourteen and a half thousand tonnes of antibiotics are sold for use in animal agriculture
2010	NDM-1 takes its first victim, a Belgian man in a Pakistani hospital. NDM-1 illnesses are reported in the US, Australia, Canada, Netherlands, the UK, Japan, Sweden, India, Pakistan, and other countries.

GLOSSARY

Acinetobacter drug-resistant bacteria that enter the body through wounds and can cause infections of the bone, bloodstream, internal organs, and urinary tract, as well as pneumonia. Highly infected limbs are often amputated.

antibacterial has had active chemicals added to kill bacteria and microbes

antibiotic substance or compound that kills or stops the growth of bacteria

bacteria microscopic, single-cell organisms that can be both helpful and harmful to people's health. Bacteria are the most abundant life forms on Earth.

Clostridium difficile (**C. diff**) bacteria that cause a gut infection that mainly attacks the elderly. Once thought to be a harmless part of the digestive system, drug-resistant C. diff can cause symptoms ranging from diarrhoea to life-threatening inflammation of the colon.

developed country country in which the income is high enough to ensure that most people have a high level of well-being

developing country country in which the income is not yet high enough to ensure that most people have a high level of well-being

DNA deoxyribonucleic acid, which is present in the cells of all living organisms. DNA is often called the building block of life, since it carries the hereditary material in humans and almost all other organisms, which determines how each organism will develop.

E. coli Escherichia coli, bacteria present in the intestines of humans and animals, where it it usually harmless. Some strains can cause severe food poisoning, especially in old people and children.

European Union organization of 27 European countries that decides on economic, social, and security policies that they have in common

gene segment of DNA that determines individual characteristics, such as height, hair colour, or other hereditary traits. Each cell in the human body contains 25,000–35,000 genes. Bacteria can have anywhere from 575 to 5,500 genes.

genetic structure genetic make-up of an organism

hygiene healthy practices, usually in regard to cleanliness

immune system the body's natural protection from a disease caused by an infectious agent such as bacteria or viruses

infection invasion of a bodily part or tissue by a micro-organism such as bacteria or viruses

infectious has the potential to cause infection

intravenous entering through a vein or veins

meningitis serious infectious disease that causes inflammation of the tissue surrounding the brain or spinal cord. It is usually caused by a bacterial infection.

methicillin synthetic antibiotic similar to penicillin and used to treat infections caused by bacteria that have become penicillin-resistant

MRSA methicillin-resistant *Staphylococcus aureus*, a difficult-to-treat bacterial infection that cannot be cured by the antibiotic methicillin

mutate change. A genetic mutation occurs when a DNA gene is damaged or changed and alters the genetic message the gene carries.

NDM-1 drug-resistant bacterial infection named after the Indian city of New Delhi where it was first spotted. NDM-1 can spread from hand to mouth. So far, cases of NDM-1 infection are few. Only one 2010 death is directly linked to NDM-1.

necrotizing fasciitis (NF) also known as flesh-eating bacteria; a rare, easily spread infection of the deeper layers of skin and tissue. Between 500 and 1,500 people get it each year, with as many as 30 per cent dying from it.

penicillin the first and most famous of all antibiotics, which acts by destroying the cell wall of bacteria

plasmid unit of DNA found in some bacteria. Plasmids can carry genes that cause antibiotic resistance.

prescription doctor's written directions for taking certain medications. Each year, doctors write more than 200 million prescriptions for antibiotics.

Salmonella rod-shaped bacteria that cause various diseases in people and animals, including typhoid fever and food poisoning. Between 696,000 and 3.8 million people contract *Salmonella* poisoning each year.

spinal tap medical procedure in which the spinal cord is punctured and spinal fluid is drained, usually to diagnose ailments such as meningitis

spore small single-celled body, often part of the life cycle of bacteria, that can be dispersed into the air

symptom sign of a disease. For example, runny nose, sore throat, and fever are symptoms of the flu.

synthetic made artificially by people; not occurring in nature

tuberculosis (TB) common and highly lethal infectious disease that is transmitted through inhalation or ingestion of bacteria. It causes high fever and lesions in the lungs. TB kills 1.8 million people a year.

Union of Concerned Scientists organization working for a healthy environment and a safer world

unpasteurized not heat-treated to kill organisms, usually liquids, such as milk and apple juice or cider; may be dangerous to drink

virus microscopic infectious agent that invades a healthy cell and forces the cell to make copies of the virus

World Health Organization agency of the United Nations, established in 1948 to promote health globally

FURTHER INFORMATION

Books

From Cowpox to Antibiotics: Discovering Vaccines and Medicines (Chain Reactions), Carol Ballard (Heinemann Library, 2007)

Drug-Resistant Superbugs (Health Alert), Lorrie Klosterman (Benchmark Books, 2009)

The Scientists Behind Medical Advances (Sci-Hi), Eve Hartman and Wendy Meshbesher (Raintree, 2011)

Superbug: The Fatal Menace of MRSA, Maryn McKenna (Free Press, 2010)

Articles

"Antibiotics in animals need limits", Gardiner Harris, *New York Times*, 28 June 2010

"Deaths from hospital bug up by 28%", Sarah Boseley, *Guardian*, Friday 29 August 2008

"Fighting superbugs", *CQ Researcher*, 24 August 2007

"MRSA and Clostridium difficile kill 30,000 over five years", David Rose, *The Times*, 20 August 2009

"The Iraq Infection", Matthew Herper, *Forbes*, 2 August 2005

"What is the NDM-1 superbug? Drug-resistant health threat explained", Katie Drummond, *AOLNews*, 11 August 2010

Websites

Do bugs need drugs?
This community education programme about hand washing and responsible use of antibiotics is directed by medical and public health officials in Alberta, Canada.
 www.dobugsneeddrugs.org

Get smart – know when antibiotics work
This CDC site provides questions, answers and information about antibiotic resistance.
www.cdc.gov/getsmart/index.html

Types of bacteria
Everything you ever wanted to know about bacteria, good and bad.
www.typesofbacteria.co.uk

World Health Organization
Look at this site for antimicrobial-resistance information, including fact sheets, technical information and news about World Health Day.
www.who.int/topics/drug_resistance/en

e-Bug
A website developed by the Health Protection Agency and European partners, where you can play games and reinforce your knowledge of bacteria and antibiotics.
www.e-bug.eu

INDEX